D0846783

the
ART
of the
VATICAN

*Anonymous: St. Peter's Basilica,
print from the 16th century,
before the completion of the
cupola.*

the
ART
of the
VATICAN

Mary Lee Grisanti

EXCALIBUR BOOKS
NEW YORK

TABLE OF CONTENTS

INTRODUCTION

This is a book about the world's first and probably greatest museum — the Vatican.

The art of the popes, collected since the beginning of Christian time but encompassing much that preceded it, is in many ways a portrait of Western history and culture. In order to illuminate as clearly as possible the human historical perspective of the Vatican collections, as well as the esthetic value and nature of the artworks themselves, this book, like the major Vatican exhibit scheduled to open at New York's Metropolitan Museum of Art in 1983, is divided into five major sections.

These sections record the development of the collections, for the most part chronologically, from the Roman tombs of the Vatican grottoes beneath the basilica, through the Middle Ages; the Renaissance, and the world-famous works of Michelangelo, Leonardo and Raphael; the Baroque period; and finally, coming full circle, the magnificent Greek and Roman sculpture collected by the curia since the 15th century.

Mary Lee Grisanti

Filarete: Bronze door,
St. Peter's Basilica

I

From Classical Humanism to Renaissance Humanism: The Bridge of Faith

*Arnolfo di Cambio: St. Peter,
bronze statue, St. Peter's Basilica*

uch has been written of "the glory that was Greece and the grandeur that was Rome," and scholars and artists have been known to mourn the fact that the first beauties and ideals of Western civilization lie twenty to twenty five centuries in the past. However, the fact is that the thoughts of ancient thinkers and the images of ancient artisans are still with us and always have been. Although the proof of this statement exists in many of the policies and ideas we take for granted in Western culture today, nowhere is there more concrete and more illustrative proof of the saturation of our culture with the enduring traditions of classical times than in the museums of the Vatican, which house much of the greatest art of Christianity. For there, in almost unbroken lines, the curious viewer can trace ideas, heroes, styles and meanings back through the centuries to the world of the time of Christ. And in this world of Greeks, Egyptians, Jews and Romans — a world of monumental building, paved roads and universal law — we can see quite clearly the foundations of one of the world's longest-lived and most powerful organizations: the Roman Catholic Church.

Only out of the immensely fertile soil of 1st-century Rome could Christianity have grown to be the pervasive culture that it became. For

*Ceiling Mosaic, Tomb of the Julii,
Christ as Sun God, 3rd century,
A.D., Vatican Necropolis*

Rome had absorbed most of the peoples and cultures surrounding it, near and far, and brought them under a single universal authority. The myths and gods of all the subject peoples were exposed to each other, changed and interacted, occasionally to be born anew.

The first basilica of St. Peter, the apostle to whom Christ gave the keys of the church and the mission to shepherd his flock, was built on the spot where the martyred saint was thought to be buried. It was a burial ground just like other Roman burial grounds of the 1st century, and Peter apparently shared it with other Roman families. But the communality of the gravesite is not so interesting as the communality of beliefs and icons.

*Tomb of the Valerii, 2nd century
A.D., Vatican Necropolis*

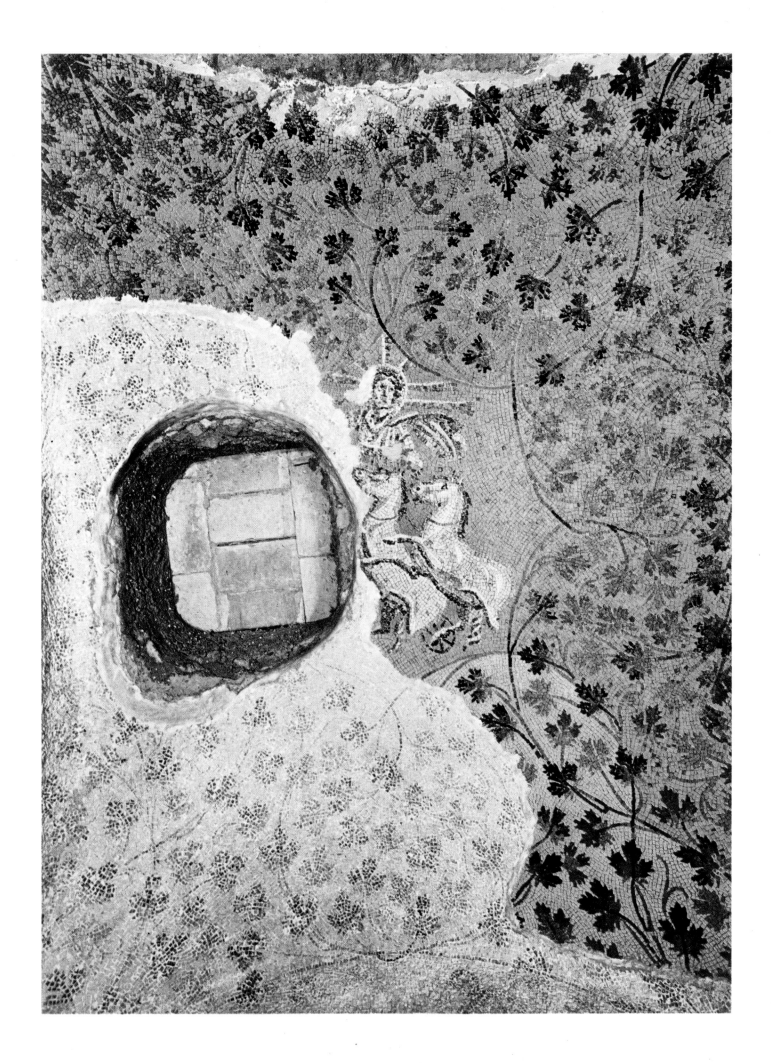

It was not unusual to see, as in the Tombs of the Valerii, or the Tombs of the Julii, which have been excavated in the foundations of St. Peter's, the worship of a combination of pagan cults. In the cosmopolitan confusion of races and creeds of ancient Rome, Greek, Roman, Egyptian and more exotic gods figure side by side: Minerva and Dionysius-Bacchus, Isis and Apollo, Jupiter-Dolichenus. But in the burial vault of the Valerii, Christian elements also appear — as inscriptions and paintings added as successive generations were interred there.

These elements are even more striking in the tombs of the Julii, in which the interiors were decorated with mosaics — an indication that the family was wealthy and could afford the best and that Christianity was well on its way to being established as the dominant faith. Still, it is interesting to remember that the mosaic which shows Christ with rays of light streaming from his head is based on figures of the sun-god Apollo (as, later, the figures of angels will be based on very early representations of Dionysius as a beautiful winged boy). The seeds of the rich iconography which constitutes the Vatican Museums, predate Christianity by hundreds of years, and through the ages Christian art will be marked by a striving to recognize and understand its roots in the more ancient civilizations of the West. For these

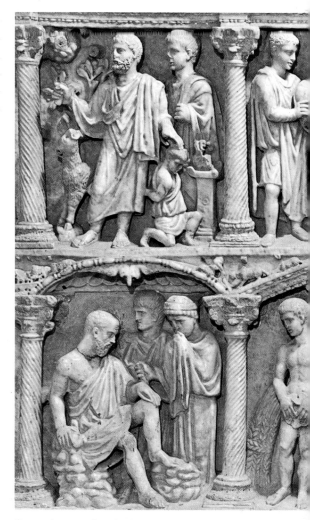

Sarcophagus of Junius Bassus, 4th century, Vatican Grottoes

15

roots would be lost, together with a great many other treasures, in the ransacking of the Imperial City many times over in the next sixteen centuries.

Perhaps the last time that classical humanism — that esthetic which posited man as the measure of all things — would be seen hand-in-hand with the Christian esthetic of mysticism and the spirit was in the 4th century before the fall of Rome and the ensuing "dark ages." In the sarcophagus of Junius Bassus, the prefect of Rome who died in 357, the bas-relief figures depict Christ and his apostles, scenes of the Old and New Testaments — but they do so in the style of the Roman narrative reliefs, and the figures are all well modeled and fully human, muscular under their togas.

In the thousand years that passed between the end of the classical era and the first intimations of the rebirth of its humanistic ideals, the papacy no doubt reached the peak of its power. In the political dissolution that fragmented the Mediterranean world after Rome, the vicar of Christ, the man representing divine authority on the earth, had some considerable claim to dominion over the many faithful and fearful. The famous Roman aqueducts had fallen into decay, and the roads were too dangerous to travel, since tribes and bands of brigands demanded their own tolls and ruled as far as their swords would reach. The prospect of uniting this chaotic world was so unthinkable that, in fact, even today it has not been realized. Yet the popes, their bishops and monks, priests and nuns, constituted a unified order that was honored in most of the world.

In the 6th century, a person as powerful as Sophia, the wife of the Byzantine Emperor Justin II, donated her own jewels for the creation of a cross presented to the pope. We do not know which pope was the original owner of the "crux vaticana," but it is a splendid and rich piece, encrusted with emeralds, pearls and aquamarines.

Detail, Sarcophagus of Junius Bassus, Christ with Sts. Peter and Paul, Vatican Grottoes

That the Byzantine empire was devoted to the Church is no small statement, either of their faith or the significance of the papacy. Perhaps even more revealing is a mosaic in the Byzantine style depicting Pope John VII (705-707) holding the Church in his arms. John VII was himself a Greek (when we speak of the "Byzantine" we speak of styles which are late Greek in origin), and he was responsible for much Byzantine decoration, especially mosaic, in the old St. Peter's.

The Byzantine style as seen in this work had enormous influence. The simplicity and stillness of the line was reverential; the empty gold background speaks of another world. It is this other, golden world, high above the blue sky and clouds of our world, that the anonymous builders of the great Gothic cathedrals aspired to, and it was this world that commanded the tribute of artists until the Renaissance.

The great American art historian, Frank Jewett Mather, said of the Byzantine style that "no Byzantine artist ever looked at a fellow mortal with artistic intent." It is clear that the spare, linear forms of Byzantine saints were never intended to be taken for real people, and indeed it was their other-worldly unreality that made them effective.

In the year 1300, a Jubilee was celebrated in Rome, and Pope Boniface VIII declared the first Holy Year. In this year the Florentine artist Giotto traveled to Rome. He had been in Assisi, where as an apprentice in the studio of the last great medieval master, Cimabue, he had helped to decorate St. Francis' basilica with many delicate, narrative paintings in the golden Byzantine style. But when he came to Rome and saw for the first time the ruins of majestic buildings and arches and their sculptured detail, he made a discovery that changed the face of Western painting. This discovery was that the essential problem of representing space in a painting is in giving the

Reliquary Cross, "Crux Vaticana,"
6th century, St. Peter's Treasury

19

*Giotto, Mosaic of an angel, Vatican
Grottoes*

*Giotto, "Navicella" mosaic, Early
14th century, St. Peter's*

appearance of three dimensions within a two-dimensional surface, that is, creating mass.

Giotto's earliest pieces in Rome, such as the mosaic of an angel, still betray the Byzantine idea of the figure defined by the space allotted to it. But the mosaic of Peter failing to walk across the water to Christ, the *Navicella,* shows an art in which space has become dominated by the figures who dwell in it. The mosaic was completely restored in the 17th century, so it is likely that the fully modeled bodies and heavily draped tunics were embellished from the simpler original work of Giotto. But the dynamic arrangement of figures, their naturalistic emotion and full-bodied form, and especially the way they command the picture space is still true to Giotto and to the principles that will, over the next three centuries, develop into the flowering of art and idea that we call the Renaissance. And though he prefigures them by nearly a quarter of a millennium, Giotto, in seeing painting in a new way, is much closer to Leonardo, Masaccio, Michelangelo and Titian than to Cimabue, his own master. In the triptych of Giotto in the Pinacoteca Vaticana, we see the elements of perspective just budding, the landscape and arrangement of figures for the first time harmonizing. These figures are not *on* the painting, they live *in* it.

By the time of Pope Nicholas V, in the 15th century, Rome had not yet developed a school of painters of her own, as Florence and some of the other city-states had done, but it had become obligatory for an artist of importance to be asked to execute a work for the Vatican. Thus the Florentine sculptor Donatello (who is perhaps most vividly remembered for his lithe *David,* precursor of Michelangelo's fierce titan) and Michelozzo were summoned to the vast building, for a decorating project of Nicholas V. Of this pope someone wrote, "He erected such a building as would have been fit not only for a pope but for

Mosaic of Pope John VII, 8th century, Vatican Grottoes

one of those Roman emperors who ruled the entire world." The regal classical aspect of Donatello's art is apparent in the *Tabernacle of the Sacrament* (1432-1433). The work takes the form of a classical temple, complete with pediment and Corinthian columns and decorated with the Greek acanthus leaf as well as urns, and the detail of the relief embodies the modeling and emotion of the new Roman-inspired art. Quite simply, the figures seem real.

Nicholas V also commissioned the Dominican monk, Fra Angelico (the "angelic" monk, so named for his blissfully colored paintings), to decorate the chapel bearing his name with frescoes. It has been said that, within the style of the new humanism, Fra Angelico expressed the spirit of medieval mysticism. There is indeed a supernatural serenity in his works. But the faces of Sts. Stephen and Lawrence and the people they encounter are immensely real and detailed, their figures are of flesh — the feet inside the soft leather shoes support solid men on solid ground. And although the frescoes are still narrative in a rather old-fashioned style, each composition is a world unto itself.

The use of buildings, as background and as a real space within the space of the painting, by which to better define and animate the figures, is particularly well handled by Fra Angelico. Note the figure of a woman, half hidden behind a corner, her finger on the wall. She does indeed seem to be half within and half outside the painting. And the use of foreshortened space, as where St. Stephen preaches to a bearded man sitting under a stone loggia, also gives a real feeling of depth — not, as in older paintings, of a figure sitting in midair above the nearer figures.

The 15th century is a wonderful period for faces. Every inhabitant of the frescoes in the Cappella Niccolina has a real, recognizable face, not the coin-stamped face of paintings before the "new" humanism of the ancients began to exert

Giotto, Stefaneschi triptych, Vatican Museum

25

Fra Angelico, Detail of St. Lawrence fresco, Chapel of Nicholas V

Donatello (c. 1386-1466) and Michelozzo (c. 1396-1433), Tabernacle of the Sacrament, St. Peter's

its influence. If you look closely at the faces of the men in one of the details, you can see wrinkles, puffy eyes, even a two-day's growth of beard! Something has clearly happened to make man as he is, worthy to be painted and displayed, rather than some abstract image of him.

Two factors impelled artists and their patrons towards a more natural, realistic, humanistic art.

The first is the ever-increasing exposure to ancient art and ideas, through the excavations that were ordered quite coincidentally as Rome began to be rebuilt out of the rubble that had lain since its fall a millenium earlier. The increasing wealth of the papacy — not only of the pope, but of cardinals and bishops who were the well-endowed sons of the rich and powerful aristocrats of other states — engendered a building boom, and as the foundations of new palaces and churches were dug, statuary, mosaic, tombs and artifacts of all kinds were unearthed. There was also an increased dissemination of classical learning through books. The first printed book to ap-

Fra Angelico, Detail of St. Laurence fresco, Chapel of Nicholas V

pear in Italy was published in 1465. Sixtus IV rehabilitated a humanist scholar, Platina (previously imprisoned by Sixtus' predecessor, Paul II), and made him the head of the Vatican Library, an event commemorated in a painting by Melozzo da Forli.

The second factor was the logical extension of the first. As the liberalism and epicureanism of the ancient ideas gained ground (as well as the more puritanical ideas of such philosophers as Plato), they began to offer appealing alternative doctrines to those of the Church. Now as never before the Church and its artists had a mission to communicate and persuade.

Part of the message to be communicated was that of power, for the political strife throughout Italy and indeed all over Europe, had turned Rome and the Papacy into a seat of increasing temporal authority, able to ally itself with such other powerful nations as Spain and France to force hegemony over its neighbors. The building programs that the popes began to undertake, the enormous projects of architecture, painting and sculpture which would eventually give Rome the

Fra Angelico (1400-1455), Fresco of St. Stephen, Chapel of Nicholas V

28

Following pages

Domenico Ghirlandaio, 'The Calling of the Apostles,'' (c. 1480), Sistine Chapel

Fra Angelico, Detail of St. Stephen fresco, Chapel of Nicholas V

face that it essentially wears today, were imperial projects, born out of motives very similar to those responsible for the monuments of the Caesars.

Within the new papal palace Sixtus had built a chapel which, like the Cappella Niccolina, named for Nicholas V, would bear his own name: the Sistine Chapel. The Sistine Chapel has become synonymous with the art of one man, the greatest artist of the High Renaissance, but it was begun by the greatest artists of the Quattrocento (15th century) — Rosselli; Ghirlandaio, Michelangelo's teacher; Perugino, Raphael's teacher; and the incomparable Botticelli.

The Sistine Chapel was built in 1475, and the frescoes adorning it have more than anything else the full sense of powerful expansiveness that was the glory of perspective. In the painting by Domenico Ghirlandaio, *Christ Calling the Apostles,* the open river view is almost like a Japanese watercolor in its sense of a mystical distance. One critic has remarked that the original Sistine Chapel, ringed by the paintings of Quattrocento masters and its ceiling (pre-Michelangelo) painted blue with golden stars, must have seemed like a modern building with a 360° view via a wrap-around window. Certainly it is the sense of open space that dominates the composition of Perugino's *Christ Giving the Keys to St. Peter.*

One of the striking elements of these frescoes, a characteristic that is to disappear in the next generation, is their mildness and restraint. Although the compositions themselves are dramatic and each individual interchange between figures reveals emotion, the overall impression is of a kind of monotonous grace. The equilibrium of the figures within their space still fascinates the artist, and perfect balance is a drama unto itself. If the expansive, architectural backgrounds seem more dynamic than the people, well, it is perhaps not too simplistic to say that this relation was also more dynamic for the artist, more mentally real and challenging than the actions represented by the figures.

However, Pinturicchio, one of the oddest and most striking artists at work around this time in the Vatican, departed from this mode entire-

31

TEMPLA DOMVM EXPOSITIS:VICOS FORA MOENIA PONTES:
VIRGINEAM TRIVII QVOD REPARARIS AQVAM.
PRISCA LICET NAVTIS STATVAS DARE COMMODA PORTVS:
ET VATICANVM CINGERE SIXTE IVGVM:
PLVS TAMEN VRBS DEBET:NAM QVAE SQVALORE LATEBAT:
CERNITVR IN CELEBRI BIBLIOTHECA LOCO.

ly. Pinturicchio's most important work was the decoration of the private rooms known as the Borgia Apartment, which includes panels depicting the life of St. Catherine. These paintings are quite exotic, almost arabesque in their coloring and detail. But though they directly incorporate elements of ancient Roman painting, they lack the freedom of form of the ancients, or indeed of the Quattrocento artists of the Sistine Chapel, who, like Signorelli display a fresh naturalism. The figures of Pinturicchio do not have muscles, or ruddy, lifelike flesh; they are wan and their movement is frozen in a merely descriptive drama in which the characters have no relation to each other or to the space around them.

But all this is to change with Botticelli. If Botticelli's figures seem mild, it is not because they lack the esthetic dynamism to spring from the painting surface; it is because they are dreaming. For Botticelli is interested not in the human form, as were earlier Quattrocento artists, but, in a sense, the human *function*. What goes on inside us is the Botticellian drama, not what goes on in the piazza or the plain beyond. In his notebooks, Leonardo quotes a wonderful remark of Botticelli's which proves that he was certainly not interested in landscape for its own sake: *"One who cares not for landscapes looks upon them as a matter of brief and simple investigation, as when our Botticelli said that such study was vain, for merely throwing a sponge dipped in divers colors against a wall leaves thereon a stain in which a fine landscape can be seen."*

With Botticelli, the interest of the humanist in man was subtly changed. From now on the human form would no longer be used merely to represent an idea or character but would struggle against symbolism and representation in an effort to become itself. The conflict between things as they are and things as they should be or might be was not just the moral conflict of the artist — it was the political and social struggle of an age that was for a few short years called golden, and then plunged into what is often called "the Counter-Renaissance."

Melozzo da Forli (1483-1494), Sixtus IV appointing Platina Vatican Librarian, Vatican Museum

*Cosimo Rosselli (?): "Crossing of
the Red Sea," Fresco, Sistine Chapel*

36

Cosimo Rosselli: "Sermon on the Mount," Fresco, Sistine Chapel

37

*Cosimo Rosselli: "Moses receiving
the Tablets of the Law," Fresco,
Sistine Chapel*

Luca Signorelli and assistants:
"The Last Days of Moses,"
Fresco, Sistine Chapel

*Pinturicchio: St. Anthony, and St.
Paul the Hermit," Detail, Borgia
Apartment*

*Pinturicchio: Episode from "The
Myth of Isis and Osiris," Fresco,
Ceiling decoration in the Sala
dei Santi, Borgia Apartment*

41

Pinturicchio: "St. Catherine disputing with the Emperor," detail, Fresco, Sala dei Santi, Borgia Apartment.

Ceiling decoration painted by Pinturicchio's assistants, Sala delle Sibille, Borgia Apartment

*Pietro Perugino, "Christ Giving
the Keys to St. Peter," (1482),
Sistine Chapel*

*Pietro Perugino and assistants:
"The Circumcision of the Son of
Moses," Fresco, Sistine Chapel*

46

*Sandro Botticelli: Scenes from the
"Life of Moses," Fresco,
Sistine Chapel*

47

Sandro Botticelli: ''The Tempta-
tion of Christ,'' Fresco,
Sistine Chapel

*Interior of the Sistine Chapel in
the 15th century (Reconstruction
by G. Tognetti)*

II

Epic Struggle:
The Age of Michelangelo

Although Botticelli and Leonardo da Vinci had been apprentices together in Verrocchio's bottega, by the time of their mature work clearly divergent paths can be seen. The detached, melancholic faces of Botticelli show a crisis that must be absorbed and endured. The face of Leonardo's St. Jerome asks: Why?

The crisis is the split between philosophy and religion that can now never be repaired. It is both an internal and an external crisis — the individual's struggle with his own conscience, and the struggle of various political powers against the authority of the Church. The career of Leonardo is an excellent example of the bitter conflict of his times. The interior man, the artist and the scientist together, probe so deeply into questions of both psychology and the physical world that we still marvel at his perceptions today. It may seem extraordinary to us that an "artist" observed a hummingbird acutely enough to describe the principles that would later be useful in the development of the helicopter, but to Leonardo the mission of the artist and the scientist were the same: to inquire as deeply as possible into the nature of things. Unfortunately this dedication to truth made him the opposite of the successful man of his day, the prince-pleaser described in the best-seller of the Renaissance,

Sandro Botticelli, "The Punishment of the Rebels," (c. 1482), Sistine Chapel

53

Leonardo da Vinci (1452-1519),
"St. Jerome," Vatican Museum

Castiglione's *The Courtier.* Leonardo was kept on the move, sometimes surreptitiously, to the courts of rival powers. And this greatest of Italian minds ended his life a political exile in France.

Eighteen years after he finished the ceiling of the Sistine Chapel and four years before he began the Chapel's masterwork, *The Last Judgement,* Michelangelo Buonarroti was sentenced to death. At the end of almost a decade of the bloodiest fighting of a war-torn century, Rome was very nearly destroyed by the armies of the Holy Roman Emperor, the Spaniard Charles V, in 1527. As the city fell, so its powerful prince, the pope, fell, dragging with him his entourage of ministers, advisers and even artists. It is no wonder that so many unfinished works by Leonardo, Michelangelo and others date from this time. It was yet other political upheavals which freed Michelangelo to complete the Sistine Chapel frescoes as well as the other great works of the second half of his life.

In order to truly understand the paradox of idealism and realism that many have called merely "Renaissance Humanism," one must first understand that the Renaissance in Italy was a time of the most extreme political turmoil. Michelangelo's Florence went through four savage reversals of government in the years from 1495 until 1530, Milan went through eleven, Urbino, six, and Naples, four.

The rebirth that the word renaissance refers to is the rebirth of the ideals and arts of classical times. Although Plato and Aristotle were the subjects of endless treatises during the Middle Ages, it cannot have escaped the Renaissance man that Plato's placid Ideal Republic was never more meaningful. New translations of both philosophers' works were now made, because the ex-

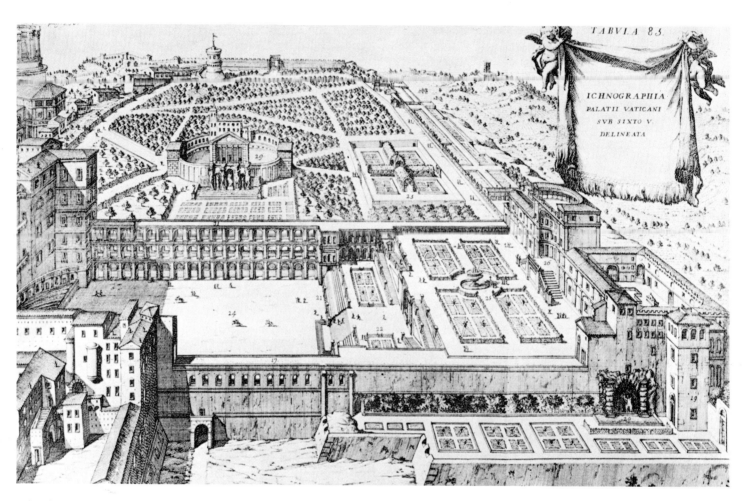

The Court of the Belvedere,
Engraving made during the time
of Sixtus V (1585-1590)

*The Belvedere Torso, Roman
sculpture of the 1st century B.C.,
Pio-Clementino Museum*

cavations that art-hungry princes made in Rome had revealed not only statues (the extraordinary Laocoon and Belvedere torso which will later appear in the figures of the Sistine Chapel) but translations of Greek into Latin as well. Before this time, Plato and Aristotle had been known only in their bowdlerized Latin versions. It is not too much to say that these translations breathed new life into ancient ideas. Where before Plato's Socrates had been a written character like the fictive heroes of Homer, now he took on a new and human dignity. To question life, to wonder openly how goodness, beauty, and truth could exist in the midst of evil, terror and immorality — the work of the philosopher — was now plainly the work of ordinary, mortal men. For Michelangelo, the ideals that Plato held out for man to contemplate were an obsession. Almost every art historian points out the violent, soul-searching extremes that are present in Michelangelo's work. They are talked about as the struggle between light and dark, flesh and spirit, religion and temporal life. It can be very simply said that in the keenly alive human being that Michelangelo was, the desire to be better, truer, more faithful to the ideal than is humanly possible was an irresistible driving force.

Before Michelangelo's time, the world of the Greeks was a kind of fantasy world. In Botticelli's famous *Primavera* we see not only the phantasms of the artist's imagination but very probably a real entertainment put on by costumed Florentines who played at being classical much the same way Marie Antoinette and her court later were to play at being shepherds. In the wistful faces of Flora and the three Graces, in their delicate feet which do not quite touch the ground, we see perhaps a kind of longing to escape into olden times as into a realm of the imagination where one can dream uninterrupted. By contrast, the broad-legged women of Michelangelo's Greek

Bramante (1444-1514) and Ligorio (1500-1583), The Large Niche ("Nicchione"), The Court of the Belvedere

59

The Laocoön (c. 2nd century B.C.), Right, original, Left as restored in the 16th century, Pio-Clementino Museum

Following pages

Antonio Pollaiolo: Tomb of
Pope Sixtus IV, Bronze,
Vatican Grottoes

Apollo Belvedere, Roman copy of
Greek sculpture of the 4th century
B.C., Vatican Museums

sybils, who are actually mythological figures and sit supporting the scenes of Genesis on the Sistine ceiling, could not be more different. There is no escape in Michelangelo's time — the knowledge of our classical heritage has made us more human, not less so, and has increased the bitterness of our longing to be other than what we are.

Much has been written about Michelangelo's early life, and while it is not necessary to go into all of that here, it is important to know that his early life was bitter and hard. He was born at Caprese in 1475 and taken to Florence where he was given to a wet nurse who was a stonecutter's wife. He later said that with her milk he sucked in the marble dust and clanging mallets that were to be the symbols of the art he so powerfully mastered. At thirteen he was apprenticed to Ghirlandaio and may have done some painting on the frescoes in Santa Maria Novella. By fifteen he was noticed by Lorenzo de'Medici, and taken into court to study antique marbles and discourse with the aristocratic society of Florence. It was when Savonarola's ascetic revolution tore down Lorenzo's utopia that Michelangelo emerged as what he was to be all the rest of his life: a stark and alienated man, without enduring friendships or any home of his own. He was a kind of tragic figure, surrounded by a wall of suspicion and hostility of his own making. He purposely attacked two of his most acclaimed confreres, Leonardo da Vinci and Perugino. He lived in jealous hatred of the magnanimous rival he doubtless surpassed — the young Raphael. His studio in Rome was said to be as filthy as a kennel, and indeed depictions of his face reveal a snarling expression that must have been habitual. The value of knowing these details is that they serve to emphasize even more strikingly the heroic, epic qualities of his work.

The imposition of the sculptor's vision on marble is in itself a symbol for the triumph of spirit and will over the mere "material" side of life. That Michelangelo's first conquest was sculpture is uniquely revealing.

Michelangelo, The Sistine Chapel ceiling, "God Separating The Light From The Darkness"

Following pages

*Michelangelo, The Sistine Chapel
ceiling, (1508-1511)*

*Michelangelo, The Sistine Chapel,
"The Prophet Jonah"*

*Michelangelo, The Sistine Chapel
ceiling, "Creation"*

The same qualities that led Michelangelo to sublimate hard cold stone into seemingly warm flesh and soft fabric are perfectly expressed by his exquisite *Pietà*. He chose a theme that was traditionally one of the most pathetic and emotional in the religious lexicon. And indeed there is in the seated Virgin and dead Christ an anguished heaviness. This is the first, the visceral impression of the statue — the slumped body of Christ that the Virgin can barely balance on her lap. But at second glance, one realizes that even under the downward pressure of the posture of the figures, the Virgin's shoulders are erect and square, her eyes are modestly, sadly lowered, but her chin is pulled in and her head is up. The message of the *Pietà* is ancient, simple and pure Michelangelo: through suffering man can attain the highest dignity, indeed, divinity. And this is a message read not only in the subject matter — the Virgin and her crucified Son—but also in the form — the solid piece of Carrara marble that Michelangelo has coaxed and tamed as if it were clay.

It is also no accident that when he turned to painting Michelangelo created figures which form part of the architecture of the Sistine Chapel. Architecture was the art *par excellence* of the Renaissance for one inevitable reason: the massive buildings of the Renaissance evidenced, more directly than almost any other form, the power and sovereignty of the person who paid to have them built. Michelangelo himself was an equally gifted sculptor, painter and architect — this triumvirate of extraordinary gifts may well be part of the reason he survived so many patrons.

Contemporary rumors had it that Michelangelo was offered the commission to paint the ceiling of the Sistine Chapel at the suggestion of Bramante, the architect hired by Pope Julius II to tear down the old St. Peter's (a church that had been the center of the Catholic world for over 1000 years) and build a new basilica which would

*Michelangelo (1475-1564),
"Pietà", (1497-1499), St. Peter's*

66

IONAS

embody the imperial grandeur and ambition of Julius' papacy. Bramante was a brilliant architect whose interest in building structure and materials as the key to the artistry of a structure parallels Leonardo's interest in physiology. To Bramante, a structure became a kind of dynamic organism —the space inside his great niche (the "nicchione") and his winding staircase seems alive. Bramante thought that painting the Sistine ceiling was such an impossible task, owing to the curved, almost Gothic vaults that formed the ceiling, that Michelangelo would fail miserably and be discredited — a typical 16th-century power play. However, Bramante misjudged the situation horribly: still stunning in both their surmounting of compositional problems and vivid originality and emotion, Michelangelo's Sistine Chapel frescoes were the most popular and influential artworks of their day.

At first, perhaps wary of the architectural snares of the Chapel itself, Michelangelo planned a restrained grouping of huge figures of the twelve apostles atop the twelve spandrels (places where two arches meet). However, he soon dismissed his helpers, whom the ceiling had rendered incompetent even to paint his first program, and single-handedly threw himself into the task. He worked on his back, paint dripping into his mouth and eyes, for four agonizing years. And lest anyone think that painting is not such an incredibly physically exhausting thing to do, it must be pointed out that the art of painting a *fresco* meant working wet pigment into sticky plaster — an aching, arduous process, since the plaster dries quickly and becomes too rigid to work. One of Michelangelo's best poems details a moment of self-revelation as he lay on his back fifty feet above the ground in the fourth year of the work and felt that the organs in his body were slipping towards his back from so many hours of defying gravity. (Michelangelo was also a poet, and his earthy, and even vulgar, writing provides an in-

73

CVMAEA

calculable insight into his art. Perhaps no one is as intimately aware of human insignificance as a painter who has laboriously dissected cadavers in order to more realistically paint anatomy. Yet, despite this knowledge, the nudes of Michelangelo are as heroic as the nudes of the ancient Greek reliefs.)

Four years after he began, temporarily crippled and with his vision distorted by the incessant strain of looking up, Michelangelo unveiled his work. We can truly wonder whether or not, dazzled as we are, we are as overwhelmed as those who saw it for the first time. It was recognized, even unfinished, as an amazing masterpiece. Even after Michelangelo had insulted his patron — the pope had asked him when he would finish and Michelangelo had replied, when he was able, so enraging the pope that he struck the artist with his cane and Michelangelo left Rome entirely — Julius begged him, bribed him, to come back and finish it.

The fresco begins with Creation, God separating the light from dark. The art historian Frank Jewett Mather has written there is no more sublime conception in painting than in the figure of God assigning the oceans their place: Here is a form that would weigh tons hovering with the lightness of an eagle in space, with extended beneficent arms as solid as reality coaxed out of the wet plaster with touch and hues as delicate as those of a Whistler symphony. (The "symphonies" of American artist James McNeil Whistler are studies in light and delicate pastel colors painted in the Impressionist period.)

Perhaps the most memorable of all the panels which span the ceiling framed by gigantic nude and massive figures of prophets and sybils, is the fresco of the Creation of Adam. It is remarkable in that God is clearly streaming with energy and Adam clearly only just able to receive it, a passive receptacle. There is something profound and unsettling in the langorous pose of Adam; perhaps, as Mather suggested, that splendid body would have been more at ease had the soul not been added.

Michelangelo, The Sistine Chapel,
"Seated Nude"

Michelangelo, The Sistine Chapel,
''Judith and Holofernes''

Michelangelo, The Sistine Chapel,
"The Supplication of Haman"

It is with his characteristic sense of dichotomy, the struggle of opposites which he so understood in Plato, that Michelangelo painted the center fresco, the Creation of Eve. Eve seems to accept the gift of life quite differently from Adam — she is eager, beseeching. Woman, depicted as the essential bearer and transmitter of life, seems to have no doubts about being alive. One cannot help seeing her in contrast to Adam. The conventional wisdom has been that Adam shows the reluctance of rational man's conscience, while Eve, mere woman, is all animal readiness for life. But this simplistic statement does not take the idea far enough. It is as though Michelangelo, rigid, idealistic man as he was, is assigning to woman in spite of his 16th-century prejudices, the responsibility for faith and endurance. It will be Eve, we may imagine, who, after they are expelled from Eden in the next painting, will first put aside grieving for their loss and get on with the business of living.

The moment that Michelangelo illustrates with this forceful juxtaposition of a man and a woman is, of course, the fateful moment in human history when our innocence was lost. Adam and Eve tasted the fruit of the knowledge of good and evil (the latter having been heretofore exclusively God's province) and, having disobeyed their Father, are cast out to make their way in a world where they must recognize and contend with evil as well as good. Though the painting shows an alternately lush and arid primeval garden and the painting is the first in the ceiling in which all the figures are nude, this new world is plainly the world of Michelangelo. And he shows his intimate knowledge of it not by the outward signs found in earlier painting — the biblical figures portrayed in contemporary dress, for example — but by internal, emotional signs. The ceiling now loses its austere godly calm. Figures writhe and struggle in the painting of the Deluge. They carry heavy burdens of household objects and hefty babies. Noah is caught naked in a drunken collapse, trapped by his daughters to

*Michelangelo, The Sistine Chapel
ceiling, "The Deluge"*

renew the human race (Eve's mission twisted and shown as an embodiment of shame). The figures in the three paintings that deal with the story of Noah are really too small to see clearly with the naked eye if you are standing in the chapel. These paintings were done first, and Michelangelo only arrived at the proper grandeur of scale by trial and error. As the other paintings have been compared to Greek sculpture, these have been compared to intaglio, the ancient art of engraving cameos.

In the ceiling of the Sistine Chapel Michelangelo tells the story of Redemption: We were created, we sinned, we have been punished, but we have survived and now wait for our reunion with God at the end of creation. But it will not be for twenty-one years that Michelangelo will attempt to depict the end of creation, in *The Last Judgement*.

Thought is divided as to the place of this work in Michelangelo's *oeuvre*. Many art critics since Vasari have found it awesome and terrifying. One historian wondered aloud at how the choir ever had the courage to sing when they had to stand looking at it. The painting, which covers one wall behind the chapel's altar, took three years longer to complete than the entire ceiling. This may be because Michelangelo was now sixty-six years old, but it probably also had to do with the theme and the frenzy which it portrays. The painting is dense with hundreds of interacting figures, all of which required study upon study to position naturally. There are so many differing emotions on the faces of the sinners and the saved who respond to Christ's final summoning that the painting is a kind of dictionary of human feeling and frailty. On the bottom left, we see the Earth convulsing and disgorging corpses from their graves. Some rise, reaching out to the arms of those who help them ascend. But on the left

Michelangelo, The Sistine Chapel, "The Last Judgement," (1536-1541)

we have largely a different picture. Livid sinners fight each other viciously and swarm on Charon's crowded boat which will carry them across the Styx to eternal damnation. Immediately above, angels or other sinners raise fists to beat down those who try to scale the sky towards heaven. The Christ is an impassive judge, his right hand is raised, his left hand falls, just so concrete and absolute is his judgement.

It has been said that Michelangelo had lost all his compassion for mankind by the time he painted *The Last Judgement.* It is tempting to believe this, for this last judgement is harsh, frantic, purposely grotesque. The artist goes so far as to depict himself as the misshapen mask of a face left dangling on a human skin held up at Christ's feet. But it may be that this peculiar piece of self-revelation is the key to the painting.

The painting has always been praised for its sheer display of power, its raw energy. In its time, this raging force won over all Michelangelo's critics and contemporaries. Yet he shows himself as a flaccid, almost lifeless (how less frightening if it were merely dead!) human hide. Remember the heavy lassitude with which he endowed Adam. It is impressive to realize that in both these paintings which earned the artist such deserved praise, he sees his own and man's place as a humble and passive one. In the midst of titanic energies — all created in the mind of one man, the artist — there is the ability to sweep it all away, to see not just some symbolic nude, but himself, as an empty shell.

Michelangelo, The Sistine Chapel,
"Christ as Judge"

It cannot be just "spleen," as some have suggested, that forces Michelangelo to portray lifelessness in the midst of teeming life. It is the tension between two opposite things which had driven him all through his life and which now, in old age, he must have felt sharply. The artist had a mission to imitate his creator — to bring forth life against a gaping backdrop of nothingness. Michelangelo, so often accurately accused of arrogance, was acutely conscious of this. Against the lavish, the squalid background of power and political intrigue that was his world, Michelangelo created biblical people, angels, saints and three persons of one God which are so real as to not be misunderstood by the least educated person. If in the ceiling he had used the physical torsion between pillar and vault to give massive strength to the seated figures that support the central panels, here in *The Last Judgement* he draws movement and three-dimensional energy out of a two-dimensional surface. It is not sensationalism, as the jaded may suggest, but sensation pure and simple, like heat or light or the vibration of sound. If Michelangelo was honored like a prince when he died at 89 in 1564, it was because he had dared to imitate a god, and came as close as anyone ever has at succeeding. He lent his immense and timeless power to the political patrons of his day: they, who appreciated power so keenly that Machiavelli has made them the exemplars of political success, must have known that only through such a creator as Michelangelo might they attain eternal life.

Michelangelo, The Sistine Chapel

III

The Birth of the Inner Man:
Raphael

t the same time that Michelangelo was at work on the Sistine Chapel ceiling, a young man in his twenties was commissioned by Julius II to paint his private suite of rooms. This young man, Raphael Sanzio, was in his brief life as popular as Michelangelo, and much easier, as a person, to love. Everything one might think of when one thinks of an artist beloved for his sweet, matronly madonnas is true.

When Raphael was introduced to Julius II by Bramante, Julius fired the painters who were currently at work on his rooms (*stanze*), one of whom was Raphael's teacher, Perugino, and replaced them with the twenty-five-year-old Raphael. The incident perfectly illustrates Raphael's career, and the difference between him and the only artists who surpassed him, Leonardo and Michelangelo. If the introspective Leonardo and the brooding Michelangelo were the opposites of Castiglione's courtier, Raphael was its perfect embodiment. And it is significant that Raphael—who was an exquisite portraitist—gave us the great and thoughtful portrait of Castiglione, as well as portraits of Leonardo and Michelangelo and other rival artists of the day whom he flatteringly pictured as classical philosophers in his *School of Athens*.

The grace and compromise expressed in the Roman rendition of a Greek sculpture, the Apollo Belvedere, are a kind of talisman for the inspiration and statesmanship found in Raphael's early work. In his *Disputa* (The Dispute of the Sacrament) there are so many traditional elements being reconciled to one another that it is only the modesty and reality of the figures' stance and expressions that prevent the painting from being a failure. But it is this sweetness, typical of Raphael, which permits a hierarchical arrangement of figures harking back to medieval art, a stateliness of pose and perspective that is pure Quattrocento, and a realism of portraiture teeming with the emotions of the 16th century.

Contemporary accounts have it that Raphael, with his superb sense of composition, arranged the painting according to suggestions of the best philosophers and scholars of the curia. His readiness to let others influence so personal a matter as composition is revealing. Unlike Michelangelo's, his work is not a vast intellectual battleground; he does not fire all his helpers, and he readily incorporates suggestions from those he has been commissioned to please. There is something in us modern viewers which finds this willingness to please repellent—we tend to admire the uncompromising works of the titanic Michelangelo. And yet there is something much more real and human in the touch of this young man who so wants to please. There is no portrait, indeed no face, among the thronging populations of Michelangelo's work that is the face of a person living in our world—these are abstract faces, with the eyes and expressions of ideas. But the merest, most insignificant angel in a painting by Raphael is a real child that one can imagine pinching on the cheek: witness the body of the dead child in his mosaic *The Judgement of Solomon*. Even the mosaic and fresco figures of abstractions, like his Philosophy and Theology, who shyly face one another across the ceiling of the *Stanza della Segnatura*, retain a girlish emotional quality.

93

Following pages

Raphael, Stanza della Segnatura,
"School of Athens"

Perhaps his most renowned work, executed when he was twenty-five, is *The School of Athens.* It is also in the *Stanza della Segnatura*, one of the pope's private rooms, the one in which he signed petitions (hence the name "signature"). This work glorifies not only the school of classical humanism, but also the work of Bramante, whose new church is the setting. It is juxtaposed to the *Disputa,* and as that painting is full of mystical elements in composition, character and detail, this one is totally devoid of the mystical and a complete incarnation of the rational. Deciphering the cast of characters is like reading a Who's Who of the 16th century. Leonardo's face is given to Plato, who gestures upwards into the realms of the mind. Aristotle is fittingly portrayed as himself, gesturing outward to indicate his (and doubtless Raphael's) natural preference for things as they are, in and of themselves. Michelangelo is shown as the pessimist Heraclitus, and Bramante as the mathematician, Euclid. Raphael, like Aristotle, plays himself; but with characteristic modesty, he shows us only a three-quarter view of his face as he gazes at us out of the picture.

It is also telling, as one critic has pointed out, that although Raphael uses Bramante's architecture as his backdrop, he takes the ceiling away, thereby stripping the massive vaults of their power to oppress and supplying the endless, liberating landscape that he had learned from his master, Perugino.

Even when Raphael devotes himself to a theme which is the most thinly veiled expression of his patron's desire for political prestige—*The Expulsion of Heliodorus from the Temple,* taken as a symbol of Julius II's energetic policy aimed at usurpers of Church territory—there is still a wonderful freedom of space, light and portraiture. And this despite the fact that he has now—like everyone else in Rome at the time—come under the spell of Michelangelo's Sistine ceiling. The *Expulsion* is full of manic movement and melodramatic expression, but the three ideas which captivate him—the human face, the interplay of space and feeling, and most important-

Raphael, Stanza della Segnatura,
"Philosophy"

Raphael, Stanza della Segnatura,
"Theology"

Following pages

Raphael, Stanza di Eliodoro, "The Mass of Bolsena"

ly, the role of light—have all become intensely interesting. Perhaps, as Mather has suggested, the whole of Raphael's paintings would suffer if the individual parts were better.

The concepts of portraiture and space as expressive elements are more clearly illustrated in another painting in the *Stanza* of Heliodorus,*The Mass of Bolsena,* in which Julius II is present at a mass when a cynical priest is brought round to faith by a miracle of blood dripping from the host. The simple spaciousness of the composition is admirably suited to the devotional content of its theme, and the face of Julius is both as real as a photograph and as solemn and meaningful as a papal decree. This is what painting could do that has been all but lost to photography.

The most significant development of Raphael's late work (it is "late" only because he died at 37) is his new understanding and exploitation of light. In *St. Peter Liberated by the Angel,* a simple and, indeed, borrowed composition is endowed with inspiration and true modernity by the wonderful use of light. The hazy mix of moonlight and the glow of dawn in the cell is suddenly golden with the warmth of light emanating from an angel. The message of miraculous grace, of freedom and triumph, is all conveyed by this light. Think of it: Light that is alive and transcends all the other elements of the composition, light created by an artist out of darkness!

Raphael's last and perhaps most interesting creation is *The Transfiguration.* Its spectacular theme of Christ momentarily revealed in unearthly light as the Son of God and witnessed by God's own voice, is extraordinarily supported by Raphael's revolutionary use of light and its complement, color.

The painting was not finished by Raphael—in fact it was displayed for the first time at the head of his coffin—but the inspiration of the master could not be spoiled by the students who painted artificial figures according to a lurid and Michelangelesque design (like the famous and embarrassing *Fire in the Borgo,* in which Raphael copies Michelangelo shamelessly and to poor

Raphael, Stanza di Eliodoro, "St. Peter Liberated by the Angel"

100

Raphael, Stanza dell'Incendio,
''The Fire in the Borgo,'' (1514-1517)

effect) and overdid the chiaroscuro, or light-and-dark foundation of the painting. The painting, like *St. Peter Liberated by the Angel,* transcends its elements to tell a story in pure light.

It is in this light and in the weird, nervous color which seems to vibrate out of the dark background of *The Transfiguration,* that Raphael has captured the turning point of the times. With these elements, in a painting largely conventional in composition, he shows that a subjective moment has arrived. The light in which we see Christ and his followers is not any natural light, and it is not the broad eternal sunlight of Michelangelo or the early Raphael. It is the light burning within the heart of a believer, a light which is not intellectual in origin but which nevertheless colors and controls thought. It is only a matter of degree which keeps this painting within the confines of the Renaissance—an exquisite restraint that Raphael observes with quintessential courtliness.

To be sure, the emotionality of the figures, their asymmetrical crowding into the foreground of the painting, and the ecstatic nature of the theme all bespeak the dizzying, dark and sensual paintings of the Baroque which will soon follow. But it will be the last time that any artist makes the grand gesture of trying to reconcile these extremes of feeling and technique with the moderation and intellect of the Golden Age. Such was the nature of Raphael, and it is no wonder that the day he died Vasari wrote: "The sweetest, most excellent painter of our times is dead." Henceforth the crisis in men's beliefs would not be salved, and the art of the Church swung back and forth on a sweeping pendulum of mystical, irrational devotion and imperial, indisputable classicism, now clearly antique. The post-Renaissance world no longer exhausted itself, as had Raphael, in trying to make its war-torn reality accommodate the serenity of Plato. Philosophy was firmly dismissed from the company of religion and relegated to the academy, and religion relied for its authority on the imperative of deep, sometimes torturous, feeling.

Raphael, "The Transfiguration,"
Vatican Museum

IV

The Power of Emotion: The Baroque

bout 20 years after Raphael's disturbing *Transfiguration,* Michelangelo painted his *Last Judgement.* Finally, it seems, he had taken something from his sensitive contemporary, a way of representing the confusing, emotional turbulence of the times. There is, as in the *Transfiguration,* no real use of perspective. Our relation to time and space has been questioned utterly, and figures seem to reach agonizingly out of a shadowy emptiness.

A passage from Benedetto Varchi's *History of Italy* describes the turmoil into which the country has been plunged. This extract depicts Florence, but the scene in Rome was much the same:

> The city of Florence when her liberty was lost was full of such sorrow, of such terror, of such confusion that it can hardly be described or even imagined. The nobles were indignant among themselves and inwardly resented being scorned and vilified by the lowest classes; the plebeians, in extreme need, could not resist relieving their minds about the nobility; the rich, worried about how they could manage not to lose all their property; the poor, day and night, what they should do not to die utterly and of famine; the citizens were dismayed and desperate, because they had spent and lost so much; the peasants, much more because there remained nothing for them at all; the priests were ashamed of having deceived the laity; the laity grieved at having believed the priests; men had become extraordinarily suspicious and covetous; women, immeasurably incredulous and distrustful: finally, everyone with lowered face and staring eyes, seemed beside himself, and without exception, pallid and bewildered, feared at all times every sort of ill.

If there is a morbidity and rebelliousness in the art that follows Michelangelo and Raphael, it is hardly surprising. For the fragmented world of the 16th century had finally fallen apart totally, and Italy was divided among foreign nations, with a rare independent state here and there.

Michelangelo:
"The Crucifixion of St. Peter,"
Pauline Chapel

Rome itself belonged to Spain, and much of its nervous, conservative Catholic mood emanated from there. It was a time when suspicion of divided loyalty could bring down the attention of the Inquisition, and Leonardo's philosophical successor, questioner of the natural world, Giordano Bruno, was burned at the stake for the heresy of pantheism. Heresy was the great and terrible byword of the times, for the Protestant Reformation of Northern Europe had split the Church irreparably.

In the face of Lutheranism, of the natural sciences now gaining in authority and raising doubts that the popes could not still, Catholicism and its art was in a crisis that could only be handled in one way. The Church was to turn away from centuries of classical thought, from a rhetorical tradition that had tried to reconcile the ancient pagan world and the rational, mathematical, observed world with the mystical world of religion. The Church was to move from being an elite center of intellectual research and artistic endeavor to becoming a body wherein the masses of questioning faithful, educated and uneducated alike, would find an awesome and irrational domain of spirituality. The new imagery and ideas were to be quite different from those of the unquestioning faith of the medieval times, though similarly based on belief exclusive of rational support. This could not be blind faith, but a faith that turned its eyes beyond the appearances of the everyday world to a world of emotions and sensations larger than life.

In the void that Raphael and Michelangelo had left, their students foundered. The dynamism of Michelangelo and the mysterious light of Raphael were distorted into a kind of sensationalism that despite dramatic, even histrionic

Michelangelo: "The Conversion of St. Paul," Pauline Chapel

112

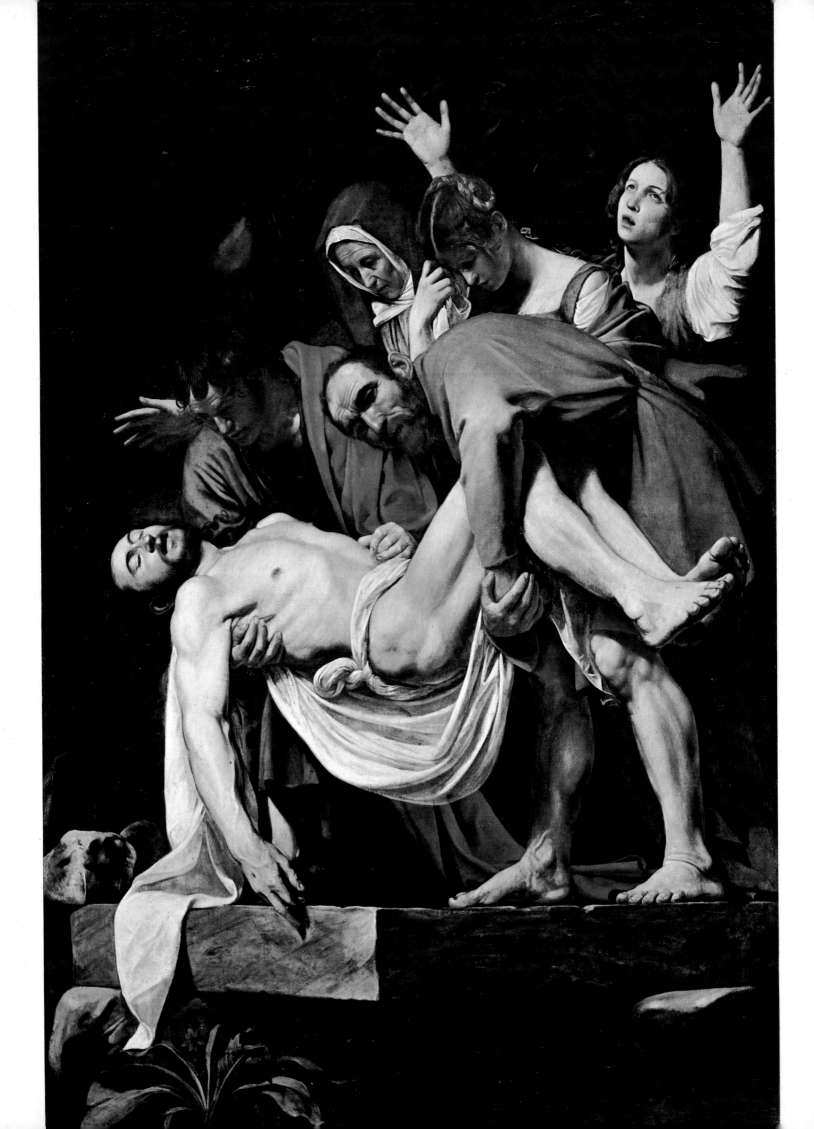

themes and compositions, is devoid of feeling. It is no wonder that as the numbness began to wear away and painters emerged who showed some originality and authenticity of vision, their work would be marked by naturalism.

The paintings of Caravaggio were both praised and scorned in their own time for his realistic portrayal, not only of the human figure and face, but of peasants, old people, women— real people clearly, not the heroic types of the years before.

Caravaggio's *Deposition* is not entirely indicative of his work—it does not exhibit the extremes of naturalism of his *Conversion of St. Paul,* which shows a grotesquely foreshortened Saint Paul lying on the ground beneath his horse, with the light of God seeming to emanate from the horse's belly; or of his secular paintings, like the famous *Card Players* in Dresden. But it does show clearly what happened to light and movement, and how these elements were entirely put to the service (as they never quite were in Raphael) of convincing the viewer of the total thrall of the figures to God.

It has been said that the shadow that envelops the 17th-century painting symbolizes man's loneliness, his abandonment by God in a hostile, meaningless environment. This seems convincing, but it must also have been seen as an encouragement to the viewer to react by abandoning himself to God. If no meaning can be made in this lonely, irrational world, it is for us to turn ourselves to the mysterious omniscience of God's will. As Calvesi points out, the more remote God is, the more anxiously he is sought.

The *Madonna of the Serpent* may have been removed from its original site in the Vatican because it was considered both vulgar (St. Anne is clearly a toothless peasant) and heretical (Catholics hold that Mary crushes the head of the

Caravaggio (1573-1610), "The Deposition," (c. 1603), Vatican Museum

serpent; Protestants, who see Mary as human and not divine, say she is aided by her Son). The issues of vulgarity and heresy could be synonymous, for not only did it upset some people to see the religious cast of characters played by recognizable actors but this was precisely the kind of popular innovation that Luther was proposing. It was, perhaps, inevitable that for reasons of expediency and policy, popularity won out, as can be evidenced in religious art until its most recent abstract manifestations.

That vulgarity was next to heresy is also suggested by the reaction to Caravaggio which we can witness in other painters. Calvesi calls Guido Reni an "anti-Caravaggist" because Reni is so clearly appalled by Caravaggio's rebellious naturalism. In Reni's *Crucifixion of St. Peter,* the faces, while real, are also stylized. The formality of the poses, because of the real modeling and rendering of the figures, takes on the weird still-life aspect of a 19th-century *tableau vivant.* Now the shadow does not seem to indicate man alone in the world, but man alone in church, in a specifically empty, devotional space.

Although the somber influence of the Counter-Reformation would continue to be felt in religious painting, fortunately the Church began to recover from the first cataclysmic fissures of Protestantism by assuming a new and transcendent stature as a world religion, respected alongside the new political boundaries that it had less and less power over. Collective Catholicism was, in its way, just as strong an idea, if not stronger, than the idea of the Church as a temporal power. And now, as the latest generation of architects were pressed to complete St. Peter's, they knew they were constructing a different sort of empire than the one Julius II had envisioned. Instead of a direct correlation to the Rome of the Caesars, the Basilica assumed an in-

Caravaggio, "The Madonna of the Serpent," (1605-1606), Borghese Gallery

117

direct relation—all the power and mass were still there, but a new, mystical, and incessantly mobile energy was indicated as well. St. Peter's was no longer the seat of an earthly prince, as much as it was the awesome throne of a mysterious and divine one. This idea plainly had possibilities that would have delighted Julius II, once he had adjusted to Luther, and a positive, optimistic and expansive spirit began once more to be expressed in the architecture of the Vatican.

After Bramante's death, his hand-picked successor, Raphael (who was also made Prefect of Antiquities in Rome, an honor reflected in the ruins that appear in many of his later paintings) began to bow to the wishes of various ecclesiastical authorities and alter the basic shape of the basilica from a Greek cross to a Latin cross. The structural dimensions of the building were changed several more times in the intervening years between Raphael's death and Michelangelo's assumption of the office of chief architect. Michelangelo, who praised Bramante's ideas and said that every architect who had departed from them had taken the wrong path, restored the massiveness and square solidity of the Greek cross. He also added a dome that with the exception of Santa Sophia's in Istanbul (Constantinople) is the largest free-standing dome in the world.

He deliberated for some time whether to make the dome a round, hemispherical shape, or to elongate it. True to the movement and restlessness of line that characterized his late paintings, he chose the latter shape.

During the 1620s, when Gian Lorenzo Bernini, the Baroque architect *par excellence*, was asked to design a canopy over the altar, he had to confront the second largest indoor space in the world. If he had tried to assume any kind of rational and classical relationship with that space, it would have defeated him. The success of Ber-

Guido Reni (1575-1642), "The Crucifixion of St. Peter," (c. 1600), Vatican Museum

nini's remarkable baldachin is that, in contrast to the massive and soaring permanence of Michelangelo's dome, he counterpoints a canopy, that while massive and soaring itself, seems to be made of wood and fabric, and to have just been carried in by a procession and set down directly under the dome. The immense bronze baldachin (for which bronze was stripped from the ancient Roman Pantheon) is something out of a caravan, with its flowering vines sneaking up the twisted columns. The top of the canopy is bronze and gold, this time worked to appear like fabric just slightly swaying with movement. It is this ability to bring movement and instability to huge and solid structures that characterizes the Baroque and makes Bernini one of its most inspired and delightful practitioners.

The Chair of St. Peter, which Bernini designed in gold to be seen through his baldachin in the apse of the basilica, was built at the height of the Protestant controversy over whether St. Peter was indeed the designated vicar of Christ. Just as the baldachin is positioned over the exact spot where St. Peter is said to be buried, the Chair of St. Peter contains and commemorates a relic of the chair that the first pope ruled from.

If the dome is the center of gravity of the basilica, the Chair is its focal point. Bernini uses the entire design of the church to draw the spectator in. There he shows sculptures (much larger than life) of Fathers of the Church—St. Ambrose and St. Anastasius symbolizing the West, and St. Augustine and St. John Chrysostom symbolizing the East—joined in upholding the authority of the successors of Peter. They physically hold the chair aloft, offering it into a plethora of golden clouds, angels and streaming rays of light—some of which *are* gold, some of which are yellow stained glass and some of which are real light from an artfully designed window in which the dove of the Holy Ghost seems to hover. It is an imperial ratification, in earth's most costly materials and most technologically sophisticated techniques, of the divine right of the popes to rule over all the Christians of the world. Bernini has realized

Gian Lorenzo Bernini (1598-1680), Baldachin over the central altar, bronze and gold, (1624-1633), St. Peter's

Following pages

Bernini, Sts. Augustine and John Chrysostom, "The Chair of St. Peter," Apse of St. Peter's

Bernini, Sts. Ambrose and Anastasius, "The Chair of St. Peter," Apse of St. Peter's

perfectly the mission of the Baroque religious artist to overwhelm the viewer with irrefutable emotional evidence of God's (and the pope's) authority.

The grandeur Bernini had created inside the church was so impressive that he was commissioned to design the facade outside the Church (the colonnade around St. Peter's square), as well as to add to the pope's residence, the Vatican palace.

The same way that Bernini drew the spectator into the Chair of St. Peter in the apse of the basilica, he now draws people from the streets of Rome, again via a design of Michelangelo's (since he designed the square), and into his embracing colonnade. Is there any doubt that the most recent generations of pilgrims who gather in the square to receive the pope's blessing feel the same sweeping, all-powerful, filial emotion that the first 17th-century pilgrims felt, standing within Bernini's endless patriarchal columns?

The Main Staircase, executed by Bernini in 1663-1666, in the Vatican palace uses the emotionality of Baroque design with the massiveness of classic formulas to humble the spectator in a very similar way. It is one of the last examples of the inspiration of Italian art, for now the wealth of patronage will shift its center from the curia to the great national courts of Europe, especially France. There are intimations of Versailles in this staircase, and indeed Bernini did voyage to Versailles, for we have his bust of Louis XIV. Empire-building would go on, but now the Church would play a different role. In the 18th and 19th centuries, the great eras of museums and collecting, the Church would turn to preserving its rich heritage of art, resting at least part of its authority on its now comparatively ancient, manifold, endurance.

Bernini, "The Chair of St. Peter," bronze and gold, (1656-1666), Apse of St. Peter's

122

Bernini, Colonnade in St. Peter's
Square, (1656-1665)

Bernini, Main Staircase, The
Vatican Palace, (1663-1666)

V

The Power of Power: Imperial Collections

O f all the structures that Bramante designed for Giuliano della Rovere (otherwise known as Julius II), perhaps none was better enjoyed, or revered, by the Pope, and by everyone else as well, as the sculpture garden in the Belvedere court.

The garden itself was an orange grove—one imagines the gentle scent of orange blossoms hanging in the air—and it afforded a view of the entire city, looking out to the Tiber valley and the hills beyond. Its collection of ancient Roman and Greek sculpture which Julius II inaugurated with the Apollo Belvedere was the most complete and famous of its day, and it has still not been surpassed.

The contemporary visitor to the Vatican's sculpture collections is struck by the sense of vigorous reality that these statues have, despite the fact that the centuries have washed away the brilliant and lifelike coloring that the ancients painted them with. How much more must the Renaissance witness have felt, for the Renaissance man lived intimately with his classical heritage. When Michelangelo and Giuliano da Sangallo rushed at the pope's request to the vineyard where the Laocoön was unearthed in 1567, they recognized the statue instantly. They had studied the Latin author Pliny, whose superlative descrip-

"Augustus of the Prima Porta,"
Roman sculpture, 1st century B.C.,
Chiaromonti Museum, Braccio
Nuovo

Stern, The Braccio Nuovo,
The Vatican Museums

tion of the statue was thought to have been all that was left of it. For them, seeing the sculpture that was unearthed practically daily in the Imperial city was like finding out where babies come from. Though artistically rich, the medieval era did not yield the same evidence of nature and humanity objectively observed as did these relics of the classical age.

As history shows, much can be made of the fact that power accrued to whomever owned such a priceless collection of antiquities. But there was another emotion involved in collecting, then as now. It is not excessive to say that these works of art were actually *loved,* as this passage from Julius II's successor, Leo X, attests: "Ever since the earliest days of youth, we have been accustomed to the thought that the Creator has given mankind nothing more important or more useful, aside from the awareness and adoration of His divinity itself, than those studies which not only serve to ennoble and beautify man's life, but which are also useful and practicable in every situation: consoling us in misfortune, and salutary and honorable in prosperity, *so much so that we would have to renounce all the grace of life and all the obligations of the community if we were without them."* One assumes that the peace and pleasure loving Leo X is using the pontifical imperial *we,* and yet generations continue to love the sculptures which play such an enormous role in opening the classical world to our view.

It is inordinately revealing that in all the political strife and social upheaval that affected Rome, including the Sack in 1527, the Belvedere sculptures were not damaged (or damaged only

133

very slightly). In fact one of the terms that Napoleon made with the Pontiff after he had conquered Rome, involved an exchange for territory and authority in return for classical art, which the French Emperor wanted for *his* new museum, the Louvre.

It is hardly surprising that a man like Napoleon would have wanted to possess a work like the *Augustus of the Prima Porta* (though this particular statue was not found until 1863). It is a heroic full-length portrait, depicting the Roman Emperor addressing his soldiers. The detail on his armor is especially interesting, showing a number of scenes and talismans, including Venus, from whom the race of the Caesars was supposed to have descended.

It is a bittersweet fact that war and political turmoil play an important role in the history of museums, and in the history of the Vatican's Greek and Roman collections this is a major factor. Much classical art was carried off by each invading and conquering army. The pre-emptive ownership by the popes of most of the pieces unearthed in Rome and the surrounding regions from the 16th until the 19th century served not only to enhance the gardens of the Vatican, but also to protect the heritage of Roman art.

Although at varying times the collections were open to the public (and when they were closed it was not always for proprietary reasons but for "decency's sake," as during the period when fig leaves were added to the naked statues and Michelangelo's frescoes decorated with loin cloths), the first public museum was not opened until 1734. It was the Capitoline Museum, a Roman museum begun with a papal gift, and it was soon so full that Pope Clement XIV opened a new museum within the Vatican.

Simonetti, The Sala Rotunda, Pio-Clementino Museum

135

In 1776, Pope Clement's successor, Pius VI, asked his architect, Michelangelo Simonetti, to enlarge and enhance the museum we know today as the Museo Pio-Clementino. He added several rooms, in a neo-classical style designed to display the works as they might have been displayed in their own times, in niches and amidst such architectural details as pediments, columns and floor mosaics. Perhaps the most beautiful of the rooms Simonetti designed is the Sala Rotunda, which was inspired by the Pantheon. It houses several of the most outstanding Greek and Roman figures in the collection, including the *Colossus of Hercules,* in bronze, the statue of *Claudius Dressed as Jupiter,* and the *Hera Barberini,* a Roman copy of a work by one of Phidias' pupils.

The *Laocoön* group, the *Apollo Belvedere,* the *Venus Felix* and many other works are still found in the Belvedere Courtyard which effectively became the center of the effort to house as many classical works for display as possible.

The defeat of Napoleon and negotiations between the curia and the French (Cardinal Consalvi was assisted by none other than the Duke of Wellington) resulted in the return of many of the works that Napoleon had carried off to France. This, of course, necessitated yet another building project, which was assigned by Pope Pius VII to Raffaele Stern. He created the Braccio Nuovo, again a hall of the neo-classical style, which was the last museum built by the popes to house ancient art until the 1960s, when the Etruscan and Egyptian collections were moved from the Lateran palace into the Vatican.

The Braccio Nuovo houses, among other major pieces, the *Augustus of the Prima Porta* and the inspiring *Niobide Chiaromonte,* a figure of a young woman running. The immense marble is all movement and anxiety—even though no head exists to give it expression, and the mood is conveyed entirely through line. Because of its superb lines, scholars have tried to attribute it to the most famous of all Greek sculptors, Praxiteles, though the base of the work seems to indicate that it was a later, though still Greek, copy.

Antonio Canova: Clement XIII Praying, Detail of the Tomb of Pope Clement XIII, North Transept of St. Peter's

Through the centuries, the collections of Greek and Roman art in the Vatican have been the focal point of pilgrimages by artists all over the world, from Goethe to Henry James. But perhaps no one expressed his rapture with the pieces, that mixture of passion and curiosity which these ancient works arouse, better than Michelangelo, in a statement on the *Torso Belvedere* which he made doubly famous through his own work.

"It was made by a human being who must have been wiser than nature itself! Too bad it's a torso!" It is a simple and exquisite regret, voiced by a man who perhaps more than any other yearned to know the creators of such works, and to know what they knew. It is a desire which still brings pilgrims to the Vatican—the museum which perhaps more than any other museum, lets us know our own past.

Giacomo Manzu: The Death of Gregory VII, Detail of Door, St. Peter's Basilica

LIST OF ILLUSTRATIONS